Thoughts and Concepts of "The Chief"

by Antonio Stitt

ISBN: 978-1-938950-46-9

Greater Is He Publishing

9824 E. Washington St.

Chagrin Falls, Ohio 44023

Phone: 216.288.9315

www.GreaterIsHePublishing.com

CONTENTS

FOREWORD

Chief Stitt has a unique way of getting the message about how to raise children across to parents, especially single parents. He uses excellent leadership skills, wit, and God-given common sense to help the parent and the child to be all that they were created to be. Chief Stitt shows parents how to alter their attitudes and actions, and as a result of that redirect, the children also change their behaviors and attitudes. Tough love is hard to swallow; so is good medicine, but the results are phenomenal.

Chief Stitt has a passion and heart to help parents understand the scripture: *"Train up a child in the way he should go and when he is old, he will not depart from it" (Proverbs 22:6 KJV).* If you train a child and make sure he or she is, first, facing in the right direction, he or she will eventually go in the right direction. When these children become adults and parents themselves, I'm quite sure that they will also use the advice that the Chief shared with their parents.

I highly recommend this book to be used in our schools, churches, and homes across America to inspire, challenge, and bring hope to parents and success to children everywhere.

All Hail to the Chief.

Pastor Rodney Maiden

FOREWORD

Chief Stitt's fresh, clear, and precise outlook for the professional, parent, or law enforcement agent has given us all a direction to follow in dealing with the future of our youth. I can't wait to make this a teaching tool in my practice and in the Church. I urge the Chief to continue to give us the solutions that yield the positive results that we need.

I salute him.

Dr. Julius Averyheart

AN INTRODUCTION:

From Whence I Came

Remember from whence you came! I have quoted this powerful statement numerous times while speaking to people about improving their lives and becoming better, faster, stronger, and quality human beings. With that said, allow me to remember from whence I came.

Looking back, growing up in the Stitt household was something special. We lived on 93rd and Dunlap in Cleveland, Ohio. I was thirteen years old. Yes, we were the typical black family of the 1970s. There were seven people in our home, which consisted of four boys and one girl, and, of course, two parents. Our mom and dad were hard-working and determined to make sure we had the skills to be productive members of society. Our parents made us do chores. It was simple; do your assigned housework correctly and you could enjoy the comforts of life afterwards. For my parents, comforts consisted of eating dinner, being able to watch TV, and going outside to play. If our work wasn't done, we not only didn't get to enjoy those comforts, but most likely got our behinds whipped as well. Our mother would have us sit on the floor around her while she read stories to us. She had these seemingly huge, thick books that were filled with stories geared for children. Sometimes, she would just talk to us about integrity, loyalty, honor, and the importance of listening and following directions. My mother talked to us consistently about growing up and becoming "champions of life." That was one of her favorite phrases. She would say, "I want you all to become champions of life."

Wow, that brings back memories. My mother would often tell us how much she loved us and that she was hard on us because she and our dad knew what it was going to take for us to be productive members of society. Our parents taught us the meaning of the words accountability, determination, and responsibility. I remember this because she made us write the words on paper, look up the definitions of them, and use them in a sentence.

Likewise, in our household, we were held accountable for everything we did or didn't do. Our home was an organized and structured environment, to say the least. I haven't said much about my dad; he was a good man. He wasn't the typical "give me a hug" type of guy. Nonetheless, we knew he loved us. He didn't read us stories or talk to us about life. No, that wasn't his style. My dad was more comfortable lying on the ground under his old Ford, repairing the brakes. One of us always stood nearby to hand him tools. Every now and then, he would say something that would make us laugh or cry–we didn't care which–we just loved the attention. Some of what I've described might sound rather harsh, but this was the standard in our home and it forged solid character in all of us. We all have accomplished the goal set before us by our parents and have become productive members of society and "champions of life."

As I grew into my late teens, and up to now, I've been richly blessed by my Lord and Savior Jesus Christ, with life coaches, mentors and friends that poured into me and helped me to become the man I am today. My parents laid the foundation of teaching me to listen, follow directions, and in all things, seek wise council. I think it's important to mention this in reference to my parents because they gave me the skills to obtain the knowledge and wisdom from the friends and mentors I spoke of. There are many that inspired me. However, in the past fifteen years, there are two that really took me to another level in the two most important areas of my life. My Chief, Mitchell T. Guyton, managed my development into police administration. He laid the foundation in developing my executive skills in managing people. In some ways, he was/is like a father figure to me. Ultimately, my Chief, Mitchell T. Guyton, taught me how to be a chief of police. For this, I will always be grateful. My Pastor, Rodney Maiden, inspired me to want to be a better human being. His teachings taught me to always be willing to examine myself first in all things. Representing Christ in my conduct, in how I treat people, is by far more impactful than walking around with my bible under my arm quoting scriptures to people. I think one of the most powerful lessons he taught was that we are not anybody's judge. It took some time, but once I embraced this life lesson, life became so much easier. I am a different person than I was years ago. I remain humble in acknowledging that my Father in Heaven has richly blessed me with mentors and coaches throughout my entire life. These people have poured into me. I wasn't born knowing how to be a good person, nor was I born knowing how to be a law enforcement officer/chief. People, men and women, coached and mentored me. I believe that if I always remember this, it will keep me humble, respectful and always ready to extend my hand to encourage, inspire and/or help another human being. Hence, this book is filled with letters and stories that you will find thought provoking, passionate, encouraging, educational and even personal. Nonetheless, the overall purpose is to share information that I believe will ultimately help the reader to become a Better, Faster, Stronger human being!

Chapter One:
Love through Sacrifice

Saying, "I love you," can be easy for some people. Anyone can say those words, but the real question is, do they mean it?

Giving of one's self, or sacrificing, is the purest expression of love for another human being. Doing something for another person, especially if it causes you to step out of your comfort zone, shows that person exactly how much you love, care for, and respect them.

When you are asked to sacrifice for another, whether it is loaning money, babysitting, or giving a friend a ride to work, the way you feel inside about helping that person shows exactly what you have for them in your heart.

You may have a degree of love or compassion for that person, but the question becomes: at what level is your love or compassion? If the situation happens again and again, will you be there to assist? Sacrificing for another human being is a great opportunity to show that person exactly what level of love and care you have for them.

When I am called upon for help, I get excited because the greater the need or sacrifice, the greater the opportunity to express my love and/or compassion for that person. I recall many times telling friends, and even family, how much I love them, how much I care for them, and I always thought they believed me and knew that I loved them.

Some time ago, my cousin was in a situation and needed help. When I was called upon to assist him, I responded swiftly and without question. He was totally amazed and surprised that I would go to the lengths I did to help him and wanted nothing in return. I say this to say that nothing is as powerful as actual "sacrifice. We all should be poised and ready for the opportunity to show our friends and loved ones just how much we love them.

Reflections:

_____

_____

_____

_____

_____

_____

_____

_____

_____

_____

_____

_____

_____

_____

_____

_____

_____

_____

_____

_____

_____

Chapter Two:

The Destruction of a Family

James and Brenda had a beautiful daughter and a wonderful son. Collectively, they developed a set of rules and instructions on how they planned on disciplining the kids. These rules and instructions were designed to teach and develop the human skills of integrity, loyalty, honor, self-discipline, and responsibility. They agreed, even though it would be hard to adhere to the rules, that these skills would be needed for the children to become successful in life.

In the beginning, the rules and instructions were strictly adhered to. Everything was going well for a while, mainly because James was the backbone and enforcer.

One day, James' boss told him he would have to work second shift, effective the following month. Concerned about Brenda's ability to enforce the rules in the home without him, he spoke to her. "Honey, you're really going to need to stick to the rules. Don't let the kids manipulate you while I'm at work."

Brenda waved her hand. "You have nothing to worry about. I'll be just fine."

The following month, James started working second shift, and that left the bulk of the interaction with the kids up to Brenda. She tried to be strong, but it wasn't long before the kids learned how to manipulate her. Whenever James was around, he noticed that the kids were getting out of hand. They talked back to Brenda and often questioned her when she told them to do something. When he saw this, he jumped all over them and made them respect her.

Alone, after the kids went to bed, James tried to coach Brenda. "Honey, you need to not let them talk back to you. You have to take away their privileges when they act out."

Instead of listening to him, she said, "You're too strict and hard on them. They are just kids and we need to cut them some slack."

James and Brenda would get into frequent arguments about this. Unfortunately, the kids would sometimes witness these arguments.

Slowly, over time, the kids came to Brenda. "Dad doesn't like us. He's always so mean."

This wasn't the case at all, however; James just refused to put up with any of their games, manipulation, lies, or deceit.

Brenda just wasn't strong enough to hold them to the standard they had agreed upon, so instead of "bucking up" and relying on her husband's strength and support to handle them, she turned on him.

The kids knew that they couldn't get away with misbehaving when Dad was around, but they also realized Mom was on their side. At school, they were taught to report any child abuse and neglect. They soon learned to use this as a weapon and would threaten to report James for child abuse.

Soon, the kids stopped speaking to James unless it was absolutely necessary. They clung to Brenda, however, and she enjoyed the attention. She convinced herself that James was the problem because he was just too hard on them.

James saw that things were really getting out of hand, so he went to his supervisor and requested that he be moved back to first shift immediately. When this happened, he arrived home shortly before the kids did. He tried his best to re-establish order in the home.

There was one problem, however; Brenda wasn't on the same page. She would often shield them from James to prevent him from correcting their behavior. James wasn't doing anything to harm them. Brenda just didn't like his method.

He simply was holding them to a standard and not allowing them to dictate the rules. This was the opposite from how Brenda had been dealing with them. Shortly thereafter, James received notification from Children's Services that he was being investigated for "domestic violence against a minor." This was a direct result of the kids calling the child abuse hotline on James because they felt that his rules were too strict. This was a problem. If convicted, James would lose his job. Actually, the mere allegation of such a charge could severely damage his reputation and credibility at work and in the community.

James had to do a lot of thinking about his life and future with his family. First, he had to determine whether he could save his marriage. He and his wife barely spoke to each other.

He tried to talk to Brenda and show her how the kids were coming between them, but Brenda couldn't see it. Although Brenda knew full well that James had never done anything to harm the kids, she chose the kids over her husband. After, several court appearances, James was found not guilty of the charges. He was required, however, to take anger-management classes, as well as parenting classes.

When this was over, James had months to consider whether or not he was going to stay in this family. In time, James decided to divorce his wife and get out of the situation. Brenda was left to deal with the kids as a single-parent from that time on.

After some time had passed of being alone, James realized that he wasn't the victim. In time, he came to understand that as the head of the household, he had a greater responsibility to protect his wife and family. James began to realize that he could have either fought harder to stay on first shift or paid closer attention to how his wife was handling the responsibility he gave her in managing the children. That would have resulted in him taking action sooner to correct the problem. He realized that, ultimately, he was the head of the family, and biblically, he would be held accountable for the destruction of his family.

Brenda realized that she should have listened and heeded her husband's advice and supported his decision. The kids wouldn't have come between them, resulting in the destruction of the family. In the end, Brenda began to think maybe she should have communicated to her husband that she was having a hard time managing and adhering to the standards they had agreed upon in reference to raising their children. James and Brenda acknowledged that their inability to communicate and compromise led to the destruction of their family.

Reflections

Chapter Three:

Good Decisions

Dear Author,

I am a single parent. My son is fourteen years old. Prior to incorporating the *Change the Parent, Change the Child (CPCC)* concepts, my son was a mess! He was in constant trouble at school, and a handful at home, to say the least. About a year and a half ago, I met with you and began implementing the CPCC concepts. I must admit, I didn't want to hear or accept the fact that I was unknowingly making major mistakes in how I interacted with my son. Once I acknowledged this and began changing me, he began to change. I mean, it was amazing. Within weeks of me setting new standards for myself and how we functioned in our home, everything began to change for the better. These changes also changed the environment in my home. It was more relaxed and stress-free. His behavior has greatly improved in school. No behavior issues whatsoever in school. (Let me stop for a second, and be real! My son has improved, but there are still issues and problems; but things are much better than they used to be, and now I do have hope. I have hope because now I have direction, instruction, and most importantly, evidence that I made the right choice in applying the CPCC concepts in my parenting style. I also took your advice on controlling his environment and watching the kids he is allowed to interact with. He has been separated from his distant cousin, Frank*, for one year. I recently found out that he had been communicating with Frank online through Facebook and Twitter for the last two months. This transpired right after his bike was stolen out of our garage, which made him very angry. My son, Steven*, stated that he knew who was responsible and that he wanted me to call the cops. I personally believed that it was pure speculation, so I did no such a thing.

I have a very busy work schedule, and I understand that bikes get stolen all the time. It would be much easier for me to just go out and purchase a new bike and keep the garage locked at all times.

Steven stated that he started communicating with Frank again because he knew Frank would help him get his bike back or seek revenge in another fashion. Periodically, I have investigated his internet activity on Facebook and other

*All names have been changed to protect the privacy of the individuals.

social media sites as you suggested I do. It had been a few months since I last checked his Facebook page. What made me check his page was the major disappointment of him being in the company of Frank when I went to pick him up from my sister's house. Steven came running out to the car. He said, "Mom, I just want you to know that I had no idea that Frank would be over here, so please don't be upset with me."

I then went in to investigate further and found out that Steven and Frank had arrived together at my sister's house, and that it was not a coincidence that they both happened to be there at the same time. Frank actually sold Steven out and told me everything without any hesitation with a slight smirk on his face. I then realized that my son had become clever and sneaky and that I had to keep up with his evolving slickness. I decided to have him log into his Facebook account. What I found crushed me to the core. I had been checking his public posts on Facebook, but I did not have his password. I saw two months of conversations that had transpired between my son and his forbidden cousin Frank. I saw profanity and talks of committing criminal acts.

My son had messaged Frank asking him to break into another kid's house in order to seek revenge for stealing his bike. Steven had times and dates of when the other kid and his family wouldn't be home. I even noticed a statement where Frank told my son that he didn't care what I thought about him, and my son, Steven, replied, "I don't care what she thinks either, F**k her!" Please tell me what I should do. Should I erase this? I did find out that no crime was ever committed, and Steven did say that this is only how he talks on Facebook. Again, please tell me what I should do.

Response

Well, before I respond, let me make one thing perfectly clear. There are no absolutes in parenting. You can do everything right, and your child can still end up with behavior issues. On the other hand, if you implement the concepts and ideas I have and will disclose, you will greatly minimize the probability of them having behavior issues. In all fairness, I think you are doing very well! Based on the age of your son when you began incorporating the *Change the Parent, Change the Child* concepts, that being around twelve years of age, he's not doing badly. When you consider the fact that he experienced twelve years of parenting void *CPCC* concepts, and within two years of

CPCC, he's improved this much, that's a good sign! If you continue with the *CPCC* concepts, imagine how much he will improve in another two years? Remember, *CPCC* is not a quick fix. These problems and issues didn't develop overnight. It took years of consistent parenting mistakes to land him where he was two years ago. Likewise, it is going to take years of consistent corrective parenting to completely turn him around. Based on the changes you've made thus far, I'm confident that you will succeed. Bravo!

Okay, let's focus on your problem. Facebook, Twitter, My Space, cell phones, and social media all can be extremely dangerous. It's unfortunate, but as it stands, you can't prevent your child from having a Facebook page. They could set up a page and you would never know it if they didn't want you to. As far as your son being clever and sneaky, there are a few things you will have to change in dealing with him. First, don't believe anything he tells you unless you can see and touch it, so to speak.

He will play on your love in order to get his way. He will manipulate you and situations to get what he wants. Your son will listen to your telephone conversations and use what he hears to his advantage, especially when you're on the phone talking about him. See, what he's doing is

23

figuring out how he can maneuver around your next attempt at disciplining him. Every time he catches you slipping or he notices a way to be slick and get something he wants, he will. Oh, and don't fall for what I call the "soft eyes." He'll give you that soft, puppy-dog look, then, hug you tight to get you to lower your guard, and then boom! Suddenly, you feel sorry for him and give in. By doing this, you're teaching your son if he whines and acts pitiful, then he will get what he wants. Can you really blame him? We all want certain things, and you are teaching him a way to get what he wants–it's not an acceptable way, but it is working for him, so why would he stop? You know I'm right; he gets you every time. Now, I ask you, is this the type of loving, thoughtful, kind child you want living in your house? It sounds like an enemy to me. Don't be angry at me. I suggested in our book, *Change the Parent, Change the Child*, you are at war with your kid, figuratively speaking of course. When your child reaches the ages between twelve and sixteen, he has developed his own agenda.

He wants to have fun and do things his way, in spite of potential trouble or problems. Make no mistake, he does love you, but his personal agenda is more important to him (at this time in his life) than his love for you.

If you have any doubts in what I'm saying, ask yourself a very simple question. Does your child know that disobeying, sneaking, lying and betraying your trust makes you feel sad and hurt? If you believe he knows and understands that his bad behavior causes you to feel sad and hurt, then why does he continue to do it? It's not his intention to hurt you, but in his mind, if getting his way results in you getting hurt, then so be it.

This may be tough to hear and accept, but it is true. Concerning his Facebook page that you have access to, you should not delete any of it. You should be studying it like the Gospel. Yes, you have cracked the "mother lode." Now, you can learn exactly how and what your son really thinks about you and everything else in his little world. Think about it. You have obtained personal conversations between him and his little cronies expressing his mindset on how he really speaks and thinks about everything. Oh, please don't tell me you are concerned about violating his personal space.

Listen, until he starts paying his own way, and providing for himself, he doesn't have personal space. PERIOD! As long as you are clothing, sheltering and feeding him, everything he has is accessible to you. This concept will

25

prove to be his motivation to move out in a few years because he'll be tired of not having any privacy. Isn't that ultimately what you want in the first place—having him grow up to be a respectful, intelligent and independent adult? You should print his Facebook pages and post them on the wall, so they'll be a constant reminder to him. Every time he sees it, he will remember the mean things he said about you and other things. This will allow him to process it in a different way and understand that what he may say to a friend isn't what he may really feel. In doing so, he may also realize that once his words are out in cyberspace, they can't be retracted and could hurt one of the most important persons in his life—you. Although he may not really feel that way, you have to make him think you believe that is how he sees you. The next time he asks you for something, you can quietly point to the post where he used obscenities and your name in the same line. I'm guessing he will hang his head as his face turns red with embarrassment. By reminding him that you sacrifice for him, he will learn this is not the best way to show his appreciation. If he continues to treat you like that, soon he will begin to miss the things you do for him and he just might even say an occasional thank you. You beat him at his own game.

No, you should never destroy those pages. Use this information to correct his thinking because now you know what he is saying when you can't hear him. There are a few things you can do to minimize his access to the internet. Instead of having internet service and a standard desktop computer in your home, consider purchasing a laptop and an air card. This way, there is no Wi-Fi service available—no Wi-Fi, no social media. The only time internet service will be available is when you initiate it by inserting your "Air Card" into the laptop. Disconnect the "Air Card" and internet service is terminated. Yes, they can still go over their friend's house, to school, or the library and go online, but you will reduce the percentage of opportunities they have to visit these sites. Although I believe this can be an effective way to minimize this type of social media, I think there is an even better way to handle this problem. In other chapters of our book, I often speak of integrity, loyalty, honor, and self-discipline. These and other qualities alike are invaluable in preparing a child for making good decisions in life.

I firmly believe that if a child is taught the meaning of these types of human qualities, and they see you consistently exercising these qualities in your own life, you will greatly reduce the probability of him making bad decisions as he grows into adulthood. Everything in our book (*CPCC*) is geared towards preparing your child to make good decisions. You may have heard the statement: "You can't protect your child from all the pitfalls in life." Well, that may not be entirely correct. If I teach my child to respect authority; treat others the way he wants to be treated; always honor his mother and father; respect his elders; be slow to speak and quick to think; to be self-motivated and self-disciplined; early to rise; eager to work and pay his own way; determined to accomplish his goals; and not easily swayed, then it may be possible to avoid those pitfalls. If I lead by example and my child sees me exercising these concepts and ideas in my own life, am I not equipping my child with the tools he will need to navigate life?

Again, there are no absolutes in parenting; but doggone it, no matter what happens, I will always know beyond a shadow of a doubt that I did my best to give my child the best chance to be successful in life. In the event that my child does screw up and is not successful, I know I would be heartbroken and sad. Could it be any worse? Imagine when I'm all alone in the bathroom and really look in the mirror at me, to examine me, and have to face the fact that I didn't prepare my child with the tools he needed to be successful. I would feel much worse. I would have to face the fact that I failed my child. I'm sure you'll agree that that would be a tough thing to live with.

You see, preparing or equipping your child with these tools will help him when confronted with the "Social Media" dilemma. When I know my child consistently exercises good decision-making in his life on small things, I can see having confidence in his decision-making on larger things such as how to handle having a Facebook page. Ultimately, with the way our society is right now, I don't think you can stop your child from having a Facebook or Twitter account, but I do believe you can equip them with tools to exercise good decision making, not just with Facebook and Twitter, but with all things.

Reflections

Chapter Four:
Leaders and Parents

Parents, you are leaders. A leader has to be a visionary and think of everything in the long term. The majority of the decisions I make in reference to my agency must be based on seeking long-term success.

My job is to manage, coach, motivate, teach, and discipline my employees to become the best employees they can be. I can't just tell them what they should do and how they should live. My conduct, my life, must mirror what I preach. They have to see loyalty, honor, integrity, self-discipline, and all the character traits I want them to have. In our agency, I tell every employee, "You must first be a good human being before you can be a good police officer."

I teach that their lives outside the job must be exemplary. They can't be liars, manipulators, or thieves, and then come to work, put on the uniform, and suddenly transform into credible human beings.

The same goes for parenting. Your conduct, your life, must be exemplary. Your children are watching you. They are watching and listening to everything you do and say. They are listening to your phone conversations, and they hear you gossiping and talking about your supposed friend. Later, they see you smile and chat with the same person you were disrespecting the night before.

They watch you in the grocery store when you keep the additional ten dollar bill that the cashier mistakenly gave you. Then, you preach to them about the importance of integrity, loyalty, and honor, and wonder why they don't get it.

Parents, you are leaders, and you have to coach, motivate, inspire, discipline, and give your children all the tools they'll need to be all they can be when they become adults. You see, you have to be the model for them to strive to be like. I have to carry myself in a way that inspires those under my command. Through my conduct on duty and off duty, I must be a glaring example of all the good that law enforcement stands for. As Police Chief, I am held to the highest standard of local law enforcement. As a parent, you are to be the highest standard for everyone dwelling under your roof.

One of the first things that I learned as a police chief is that, ultimately, my police agency took on my personality. If I am reasonable, honest, fair, and patient, then my officers will see and respect those traits and model themselves after their leader.

Likewise, if I were to get a kick out of causing confusion, pitting people against one another, lying, manipulating and taking advantage of others, abusing my power and authority, or did not care about being fair to people, then the personality of my agency would eventually reflect the same. It would be an office of chaos and not one I would be proud of at all.

Think about it; if this were the case, when a corrupt chief is informed of an employee lying, manipulating, being unfair to others, abusing his or her power and authority, that chief will not be bothered or concerned because he or she will be comfortable with it.

On the other hand, if the chief has integrity, loyalty, honor, self-respect, cares about being fair to others, does not manipulate or take advantage of others, and he or she is informed of an employee behaving in a way that misrepresents his or her personality, it will not be tolerated.

Likewise, in our book, *Change the Parent Change the Child,* we talk about the importance of how the parent's behavior impacts the behavior of the child. The child is simply an unpolished version of the parent. This statement, which is taken from the *CPCC* book, is saying that the child will emulate the personality of who they are around the most, which in most cases, is the parent.

Reflections

_____

_____

_____

_____

_____

_____

_____

_____

_____

_____

_____

_____

_____

_____

_____

_____

_____

_____

_____

_____

_____

_____

Chapter Five:

Not Knowing

None of us were born having all the answers. We live, we learn, we grow. The *CPCC Movement* embraces this concept. In Proverbs 12:15, a wise, noble man once said, *"A wise man, seeks wise council."*

The second we begin to believe we don't need to improve anymore, or that we don't need to listen anymore, that second...we actually begin to regress. When someone goes to school and achieves the educational level of doctorate, don't they periodically go back for updates? We never stop learning. There is always room for improvement, or at the very least, we have to keep training to maintain that educational level because time never stops. Likewise, neither does knowledge.

If everything around you is evolving, shouldn't you? When you stop seeking to become better, stronger, or faster, you will eventually stop, period.

The *CPCC Movement* does not fault the parent for not knowing how to teach a boy how to be a man and gentleman nor to teach a girl how to be a woman and lady. You will be held accountable, however, for continuing to not know once you are given the information. Once you've acknowledged that you have a deficiency in your parenting skills, you have an obligation to seek help. Your child's future is at stake. If you don't correct the problem, you are failing as a parent, and most importantly, you are failing your child and increasing the probability of them growing up with similar deficiencies or worse!

Please know that it is not my intention to offend or talk down to anyone, but I can't change the truth. I believe you would rather have me be honest than to lie and pretend you don't have a problem or that the problem lies with your child or someone else. The reason our youth are in the condition they are in today is because nobody has taken responsibility and ownership for their role in how things got this way. *CPCC* understands and acknowledges that parenting is not easy and that a good parent will thirst for the knowledge to become a great parent and role model. Some of the character traits a child will need to be successful are integrity, loyalty, humility, respect for authority, self-motivation, self-discipline, courage, truthfulness, intelligence, self-respect, honor, and biblical or spiritual beliefs. These are just some of the qualities that will assist in the positive development of your child.

Remember that you, the parent, are your children's greatest influence. They are going to emulate whoever they are around the most. If that person is you, then I would venture to ask one question. Do you possess at least six of these character traits? Whatever your answer is, know that the *CPCC Movement* represents hope. We were established because we firmly believe that it all starts with the parent.

When your children were infants, you provided everything they needed. If they needed milk, you gave them milk. If they needed food, you gave them food. If they needed comfort, you held them. As they grew, whatever they needed, you provided. You were in control of everything in their lives because they couldn't provide for themselves.

So what happened? The parenting concept standards have plummeted in our country. The *CPCC Movement* has been established to raise the standards of parental control, which we at *CPCC* believe will be the catalyst in changing a generation of children and, equally important, their parents.

Reflections

_____

_____

_____

_____

_____

_____

_____

_____

_____

_____

_____

_____

_____

_____

_____

_____

_____

_____

_____

_____

Chapter Six:
Parental Accountability

A few years ago, police officers were horrified over a video tape showing two preschoolers smoking marijuana. The kids were being coached on how to smoke by their own teenaged uncle. In one part of the video, it appeared that the seventeen-year-old uncle and another eighteen-year-old man were persuading one child to smoke and actually held the marijuana cigarette for the toddler. Later, a different child was taped smoking by himself. Both men were later charged with third degree felonies.

When most people hear about something like this, the first thing they ask is, "Where were the parents?" This incident occurred in the children's home, not in a back alley. After viewing the tape, the children's mannerisms led the police to conclude this was not the first time the kids had smoked. The mother was sleeping in an upstairs bedroom when the incident occurred. This is a case where the parent, even though she was asleep, should be held accountable and charged criminally.

Parental accountability is an effective way of dealing with the problem, but is it the only way? Dr. Sebastian Kraemer says, "In the past few years, spurred on by increasing anxiety about juvenile violent crimes, delinquency, and drug abuse, public debate about the contribution of parents has become more intense. This said, it is tempting to blame parents for the bad behavior of their children, but this is a more thought-provoking discussion than one might think." Across the nation, more cities and state laws are being made and upheld to hold parents accountable for their children's actions. The Parental Liability law suggests that young people are not fully responsible for their actions.

In parenting, the word, *accountability*, can be a subjective word by its very nature. The following scenario shows the subjective nature of accountability: A father purchases a handgun and keeps it safely out of harm's way in a firearm lockbox, lawfully secured by a key. The location of the key is unknown to other family members. Later that same year, his sixteen-year-old son is involved in a physical altercation with another teenage boy at school.

The son runs home, still upset about the outcome of the incident. He searches for his father's key but is unable to find it, so he decides to break it open. Grabbing the gun, he goes back to the school and shoots and kills the boy. Should the father be held accountable for the actions of his son? After all, the gun did belong to him and he did bring it into the home. Should he be held accountable purely because he kept a firearm in his home, or should the sixteen-year-old son be held accountable for breaking into the secured lockbox, and with premeditation, using the gun to take the life of another?

The father is responsible for the actions of his son simply because he is the parent of a minor under the age of eighteen. At what point does society hold the teenage son accountable for his actions? The Young Offenders Act of 1994 set out in the Declaration of Principle states, "Young people are to take responsibility for their actions. It is inappropriate and counterproductive to send such a confusing message to young people and their families. If parents are held accountable as well as or instead of the young person, young people will not learn to take responsibility for their actions and will be less likely to alter their behavior." Having said this, one must consider that the idea of holding the parent accountable or responsible can have many different variables.

A parent can be responsible for the actions of their child and not actually be *accountable*, which is different than holding a parent *accountable* and can have many different variables. A parent is responsible for the child's health, welfare, education, and overall well-being until the age of eighteen. When the child commits a crime, the parents must be able to legally prove that they have done everything in their power to control the child's negative behavior or prevent a crime from being committed.

A teenage daughter, who is consistently in trouble with the law, disappears for weeks at a time. The mother tries her best to prevent her daughter from leaving and tries to find her every time she leaves, but she does not have a clue about where she might be. Although the mother does not condone this behavior, she is still responsible and accountable for anything her daughter does until she reports her to the authorities as unruly or incorrigible. At that point, the mother remains responsible in that she would have to represent her daughter in any matter that occurred, but she is no longer accountable for what her daughter may do.

When the mother reports her daughter as incorrigible, she is admitting that she can no longer control the behavior of her daughter and cannot, in good conscience, be blamed for where she is or what she does. This, consequently, releases the mother from any accountability of the daughter's actions. In this instance, if a crime was committed by the daughter, the mother would have to appear in court as the representative of the daughter, but the daughter would face the charges and suffer the consequences for the crime. The American Civil Liberties Union of 1996, states that "Parenting responsibility laws are a 'quick fix' approach to juvenile crime that fails to address the underlying problems." Of course, poor parenting skills certainly can have an adverse effect on the behavior of developing teens. There are a number of circumstances that can affect the way a child responds to the parent. Is there abuse or neglect in the home? Is there excessive discipline? Parents may just be at their wits' end, and they don't know what else to do to make the child behave. Some parents may not understand that giving a child everything they want is not a good idea. They don't want their kids to be mad at them, so they give in. Unfortunately, all that teaches the child is instant gratification feels nice. Studies have shown that there are a number of issues which carry the potential of severely affecting the parenting methods in the home. One must remember that in spite of the enormous responsibility that is placed on parents, they are also human and subject to error. Poor parenting can be the result of many different things. It's important to look at the entire picture. Is there undue stress in the home? Was the parent abused as a child? Are there financial problems? All of these situations can result in poor parenting choices. Yes, parents should be held accountable for the actions of their child. However, research shows that there are circumstances which can reduce or eliminate the accountability of the parent.

The attitude towards parenting can determine how effective the methods are. For the parent, it can be a unique opportunity and responsibility. The opportunity is in being given the privilege to have a completely new and untouched life, to mold and develop into adult maturity through the wisdom and knowledge the parent has developed from their life experiences over a period of time. Likewise, the responsibility is in preparing the child for life by instilling human qualities such as integrity, loyalty, responsibility, humility, self-discipline, and the ability to listen more and talk less. These are the tools the child will need to become a productive and successful member of society.

Reflections

_____

_____

_____

_____

_____

_____

_____

_____

_____

_____

_____

_____

_____

_____

_____

_____

_____

_____

_____

_____

_____

_____

Chapter Seven:
"Police Executive Leadership"

An executive leader is a unique position. The executive leader (E.L.) must think and process everything differently. His or her plans are almost always long term. Executive leaders rarely give up on an idea. They are always thinking of ways to get it done. Even when there are obstacles, they will immediately begin to search for ways to overcome whatever is impeding the accomplishment of their goal or objective.

Some of the essential qualities of an effective E.L. consist of team building, long-term planning, motivation, discipline, and teaching. A team builder will bring people into the agency with a mindset and attitude that will fit the objective and direction of the agency. Likewise, he or she must be ready to remove an employee that consistently fails to meet the standard.

If an employee falls below the standard, his or her behavior will infect other employees. Eventually, this will prove to be the catalyst of negativity and create disgruntled employees in the agency. Having said this, sometimes the executive leader has to be able to recognize when there could be a personal issue or problem that an employee could be having which may or may not be job related. This situation may require compassion. The E.L. will have to be able to determine how far he or she is willing to go to help that employee so as not to jeopardize the credibility or standard of the agency.

The E.L. must be able to plan for the long haul. One way of long-term planning is investing in the agency by building a strong team, which takes years to accomplish. The position of executive leader requires a visionary mindset.

It's kind of like he or she is sitting high on top of the mountain, looking down at all areas of the agency, which gives a full panoramic view. This enables the executive leader to make decisions and address issues in ways that his or her staff may or may not understand because the executive leader's viewpoint is different from those under his or her command.

There will be times that the leader will need to motivate his or her team. By knowing the people he or she is speaking to, the supervisor should have a better feel for the pulse of the agency. This information will give the executive a good idea of how to motivate the team.

In the event that the E.L. needs to speak to an individual person but doesn't know that employee personally, the E.L. should make sure he or she has an opportunity to meet the employee and be able to get a feel for the employee's personality from the conversation, as well as the body language and the attitude the employee exudes. After this, the leader should be able to surmise what words will motivate and inspire that employee to perform to the best of his abilities.

Periodically, I bring individual officers into my office and allow them to discuss anything that might be on their minds. Whether it is job related or personal concerns, I sit back and give the officer my undivided attention. During this hour or so, I learn important things about my employee. Using the knowledge I've gleaned, I am then able to motivate, encourage, and, if needed, discipline this employee based on my listening and giving my full attention. Furthermore, this gives the person a feeling of importance because I took the time to acknowledge and validate my employee. This is vital in building a strong team.

Discipline is another important quality for a leader to have because the executive sets the standard in how the agency will function. Once the standard has been established, it must be maintained and adhered to. However there will be instances where the executive leader will need to know what level of disciplinary action to impose in a situation. He or she can't function under the mindset of slaying anyone who dares to violate the standard.

The executive leader has to have the ability to examine every situation or incident, and determine whether or not this employee was trying to do his or her job but simply made a mistake or if the infraction was a result of an arbitrary employee with a personal agenda who failed to follow instructions. Although both of these situations resulted in a violation of departmental standards or policies, I believe they would require different levels of disciplinary actions.

Another extremely important concept in disciplining employees is consistency. Discipline must be consistent and fair; if it isn't, then in many cases, the disciplinary action could destroy morale in the agency as well as the respect that employees are supposed to have for the administration. Discipline is like holding a double-edged sword that doesn't have a handle. You have to wield it carefully or it will cut you as well as the employee.

The final quality is a coach or teacher. I believe this quality is equally if not more important than all the others. The executive leader has to know how to coach and teach those under his or her command. To do this requires patience, wisdom, understanding and lastly, humility.

Humility, will always remind executive leaders that they didn't always have the knowledge that they now possess. Someone had to take the time to teach them. Having said this, the same patience, wisdom and understanding should be implemented in the executive leader's method of coaching and teaching. As I put these opinions to print, I recalled another quality which I believe to be imperative in the character of the effective executive leader.

That quality is referred to as presence. The executive leader is the pinnacle of the agency. He or she is the one from which everyone else draws strength, confidence, and knowledge. Given that, your mere presence should display confidence and poise. In doing so, executive leaders encourage those under their command to respect, admire and trust their ability to lead.

This can be a difficult task considering you don't want to appear arrogant or unapproachable. There is a fine line between the character traits of confidence and arrogance. The executive leader has to find that line and live on it for the good of the agency. I have great respect and admiration for this position. I believe it takes a special human being to don the title of an executive leader.

Reflections

_____

_____

_____

_____

_____

_____

_____

_____

_____

_____

_____

_____

_____

_____

_____

_____

_____

_____

_____

_____

_____

Chapter Eight:

Prestigious

During the years of research and development of the *CPCC* book and movement, I came across many interesting parenting dilemmas. There is one dilemma that has always stood out for me. I want to stress that this situation is being shared to educate you, the parent, not to ridicule or make fun of anyone.

One day, a Mrs. Beck* contacted me and asked, "Can my husband and I come to your office to discuss a problem we have been having with our son?"

I agreed to meet with them, and shortly thereafter, they came in to see me. After sitting down and exchanging pleasantries. We got to the heart of the matter. Mrs. Beck furrowed her eyebrows as she spoke. "Our son, Mike, is constantly in trouble in school. His grades aren't horrible, but he could do so much better. Everyone says he has potential but he doesn't apply himself."

Mrs. Beck looked at her husband. He nodded as he

*All names have been changed to protect the privacy of the individuals.

spoke. "My son is so bad that the school administration has tagged him a troublemaker."

For roughly forty minutes, both parents talked about specific incidences where Mike made bad decisions, acted inappropriately, and how the people at school viewed him.

Finally, I held up my hand to stop them and asked, "What can I do to help?"

Mr. Beck took a deep breath and then exhaled. "A close friend has offered to discreetly enroll Mike into one of the best schools in the county. It's for students who are quite bright and usually make the honor roll at their own schools." Mrs. Beck sighed before saying, "This is a great opportunity for our son. They have a zero tolerance for bad behavior. He'll be in the best school, with the best kids. We're so thrilled that Mike has this opportunity to attend this prestigious institution. What do you think, Chief?"

At this point, I took a deep breath in and exhaled slowly as I gathered my thoughts. "Okay, let me mirror back to you what I'm hearing thus far. Your son is presently attending a regular junior high school in the community. Because of his consistent poor behavior and lackluster grades, he's considered a troublemaker in school. Now, you've been given the opportunity to discretely enroll your son who, by the way, is still a troublemaker and still brings home subpar grades, into one of the most prestigious institutions of learning in this county."

Mrs. Beck said, "Chief, you don't understand; we believe our son's behavior will change when he is around better quality kids and higher standards."

I held up my hand. "You came here for my advice, correct?"

They both nodded and Mrs. Beck said, "Yes, Chief Stitt, we want your honest opinion. What do you think we should do? After all, this is a wonderful opportunity." She tilted her head and smiled as if she could get me to say what she wanted to hear.

I leaned in and spoke calmly, enunciating each word to make sure they heard me. "Okay, I believe you will be setting your son up for failure. I think you are taking a major risk with your son's future. I listened to you both, and it sounds more like you are equally, if not more, excited about being able to tell your friends that your son is attending one of the most prestigious schools in the county."

"If your son isn't meeting the standard at the school he is presently attending, what makes you think he will be able to meet an even higher standard elsewhere? Is it that you both believe he can do better but chooses not to?"

Both Mr. and Mrs. Beck turned to look at each other and smiled. Mr. Beck answered, "Yes, absolutely; we know he can do better, but he just doesn't try hard enough."

Shaking my head, I looked at them and raised my eyebrow. "Really, why do you tolerate those actions if you know he can do better?"

Suddenly, they looked at each other, but neither one said a word.

"Listen, your son is not accustomed to following rules and functioning in an organized, structured environment. The school you are considering is not going to tolerate his antics at all. Within a couple months, he'll be in trouble there just like he is now. His grades will plummet because that school won't tolerate his excuses for not getting his work done."

"Both of you need to raise the standards in your home first. Ask yourselves if the environment at home is organized and structured. If not, start there. Establish a zero tolerance policy for bad grades and inappropriate behavior at home or at school. Yes, this is a nice opportunity; however, neither your son nor you are ready yet. Have you given any thought to how destructive it would be if he fails or gets expelled? It could destroy his confidence and make him believe that he is a complete failure.

"I know you love your son, so in loving him, why take that chance with his future? I can see that this is a tough decision for you both. I think you love your son and want only the best for him. Right now, you have to sacrifice your time, intelligence, understanding and wisdom to improve the mindset of your son. The *CPCC Movement* will provide you with doable instructions, scenarios, true stories, and information on how to accomplish this goal."

This real-life experience can help all parents understand what their children need from them.

I understand and acknowledge the fact that parents ultimately want the best for their children. I've witnessed parents who know full well that their children are unruly, disrespectful, and overall troublemakers; yet, they chose to ignore this fact and left family members, friends, teachers and fellow students vulnerable to their children's tyranny.

I challenge you parents to ask relatives, friends, and educators for an honest opinion of your children's behavior. First, mentally remove the blinders and extract the ear plugs. You have to be willing to lower your guard and try not to become defensive if they say things you don't want to hear. If they are being honest, it's more likely that some of their words might sting a bit. Remember, this is to help your child, not massage your ego. If you're really honest with yourself, you know what they might say is basically true because you live with "Little Egghead," and you spend a great deal of time yelling, repeating instructions, debating issues, and enduring consistently poor behavior at home, but you have deluded yourself into believing it's not that bad.

Stop it. Be willing to face the truth for the long-term sake of your children. If you know your children lie to you, manipulate situations, do not follow instructions, and do not respect authority, what are you doing about it? In a few years, they should be looking to get out on their own. With these personality issues, what employer is going to hire them? If they are able to secure employment, how long do you think they'll last when things don't go their way?

Listen, you have to stop the bleeding by, first, examining yourself. Make sure your parenting skills are conducive for long-term success.

Second, make sure the environment in your home is equally conducive for success. There shouldn't be any yelling in your house by anyone–parent and child alike. Have your children perform daily chores such as making their beds, washing dishes, cleaning the bathroom, mopping the floor, and picking up their rooms. Likewise, if you don't challenge them a little, they will never grow and be able to see their progress.

Most kids should be able to hang up and or fold their clothes when they return home from school. Also, there should be consistent spiritual and biblical training by everyone, including parents. This will assist greatly in setting boundaries and accountability. All of these things establish structure and organization in children's lives.

Third, these standards and policies have to be strictly enforced. You couple this with love and compassion, you'll be well on your way to preparing your children for long-term success.

Reflections

_____

_____

_____

_____

_____

_____

_____

_____

_____

_____

_____

_____

_____

_____

_____

_____

_____

_____

_____

Chapter Nine:

The Effective Leader

The head of a household is a leader. Being a leader is a great opportunity, honor, privilege, and most of all, a responsibility. The leader of the household has to consistently exhibit a behavior that gives those under his or her command reason to believe he or she is qualified to lead the family.

I am a single mother of two children, a boy and a girl. Can I be an effective leader?

I often hear questions like the one above, and the answer is a resounding yes!

The effective leader of the household teaches, motivates, inspires, makes decisions geared towards long-term success, and consistently provides a glaring example of what it takes to be successful in life. The effective leader has the ability to make tough decisions and huge sacrifices for the betterment of everyone, even when nobody agrees. In situations where the father is not active or present in the home, the mother has to take on that role. In order to be an effective leader, it is vital to establish a firm foundation for the family. This is done not only by teaching kids the meanings of certain words, but also by living out these attitudes in your own life. It's important for kids to understand what words like integrity, loyalty, honor, self-respect, self-discipline and determination mean. Teach them how to apply these character traits in everything they do. The best way to show kids is to apply these traits to every aspect of your life. You'd be surprised how much kids pick up on things, even when we don't think they are watching us.

Although doing this will prove to be valuable to them, it is not enough. At some point, probably between the ages of thirteen and fifteen, a son needs to have a male mentor. The mother needs to seek out a person whom she trusts and believes is qualified to teach her son how to be a man. This can be a tough call for a mother because she will have to relinquish some of her authority over him to the mentor. She will have to trust his judgment over her own (in some areas). During the early to mid-teen years, the son (generally speaking) will test her. Think about it; his voice is changing. He's getting bigger, taller, and stronger. At this point, the

64

natural progression is for a young man to want to challenge. This can be a healthy time for him if he has been raised correctly prior to this time. This is where the male mentor will be extremely instrumental in dealing with the young man's aggressive attitude. The male mentor can prove valuable in helping the mother understand the changes that the young man will be experiencing, as well as how to respond to them.

The daughter, on the other hand, is a little different. The mother, who is the effective leader, must be a walking, breathing example to her daughter of how to carry herself like a lady. The mother's interaction with males will ultimately be the daughter's blueprint of how she picks her mate. The daughter will emulate who she is around the most. In most cases, if the mother sets a high standard for herself, so will her daughter. She needs to be aware that her daughter is watching how the mother dresses, speaks, carries herself, and maintains and organizes her life. Most importantly, the daughter will be acutely aware of the way her mother interacts with men. To be an effective leader, the mother may want to ask herself, "Would I want my daughter to do this, wear this, or behave like this?" If the answer is no, then the mother should avoid those things so that she becomes a good role model for her children. Her daughter is watching and listening to everything her mother says and does. If, as her mother, you allow her to be in the company of men who consistently drink alcohol or use other mind-altering substances, you are unknowingly setting an example for the type of man your daughter will date because that is the type of man she feels used to or is comfortable with. The more she sees that type of behavior, the more normal it becomes to her. If you allow a man to physically or verbally abuse you, your daughter might believe that is how women should be treated. Likewise, a son might think that is how a man treats a woman, so he may grow up to abuse you and girls he dates as well. I'm not trying to make any negative comments about anyone drinking alcohol or using drugs. I simply used that as an example. If you don't think you would be concerned if your daughter came home with a guy who appeared to have been drinking or was high, that's totally up to you. I'm just giving information about what can happen in some cases, but certainly not in every situation. Ultimately, when you are an effective leader, how you carry yourself at all times is as important as what you have to say. If you are confident, positive, and motivated, rarely will you be let down or at a lost.

Reflections

_____

_____

_____

_____

_____

_____

_____

_____

_____

_____

_____

_____

_____

_____

_____

_____

_____

_____

_____

_____

_____

Chapter Ten:

Change the Parent, Change the Child (A Sad Commentary on our Society)

On a nice, sunny afternoon, Johnny Jr. was watching the baseball game in his bedroom. His mom was preparing dinner in the kitchen and also watching the game. Both Johnny Jr. and his mom had a special interest in this game because Johnny's dad was playing in that game. This was only the second time Johnny Jr. saw his dad play on TV. It was in the third inning and Johnny's dad was up at bat.

The pitcher threw a sizzling fastball, low and inside. The umpire dramatically yelled, "Strike!"

John slammed his bat on the plate three times as he glared at the umpire and then stepped back out of the box. The crowd picked up on John's attitude and started booing the ump. John stepped back in the batter's box and got ready for the next pitch. He was preparing to knock the cover off of this one. As the ball left the pitcher's hand, he could see it coming right at him, almost in slow motion. He leaned back a bit to shift his weight on his back leg so he could really smack this one. He swung with all he had, but hit absolutely nothing. The pitcher had tricked him into swinging at a sinker. The ball had sailed right towards the middle of the plate. John's mouth watered as he watched the ball coming right at him. Just before the ball reached the plate, it dived straight down, and his bat missed the ball by mere inches. The ump screamed, "Strike two!"

The pitcher smiled at Johnny's dad because he fooled him again. This just made John angrier, and he really wanted to show that pitcher that he could hit his pitch. He stepped back into the batter's box and got ready for the next pitch. The pitch came quickly, and John lost sight of the ball, so he just swung wildly. He hit nothing. The ump screamed, "Strike three, you're out!"

Johnny's dad stomped back to the dugout, took his helmet off and hurled it to the ground. When he reached the dugout, he took his bat and started smashing water coolers, chairs, helmets, and whatever else he could swing at. All of this was captured on video and shown over and over on all the TV stations. Of course, Johnny Jr. saw this clip many times.

A few weeks later, Johnny Jr. and his mom were watching his dad in another game. Again, he struck out. It shouldn't have been a big deal because most players get out more often than they hit the ball, but Johnny's father didn't care if it was normal. Once more, he threw a temper tantrum. He smashed everything in sight. Again, his son, Johnny, saw it all.

Not long after that, one afternoon, Johnny decided he wanted to go outside and play. He grabbed his coat as he headed towards the door.

His mother looked up and said, "What are you doing? You can't go outside without asking. Plus it's getting late, and I don't want you to go out."

Grumbling under his breath, Johnny stomped off to his room. Moments later, his mother heard all kinds of bumping and thumping. She went to his room and saw Johnny Jr. with his Louisville Slugger baseball bat smashing up everything in his room.

His mother grabbed him and sat him down. "What in the world are you doing? Why are you smashing and breaking all of your things?"

Johnny looked at her with a surprised look on his face and shrugged his shoulders. "I'm just doing what Dad does when he gets mad, and I was mad that you wouldn't let me go outside. What's the big deal?"

Just because our society approves of a certain behavior, it doesn't make it right. Parents cannot let society dictate how we are going to raise our children.

Reflections

_____

_____

_____

_____

_____

_____

_____

_____

_____

_____

_____

_____

_____

_____

_____

_____

_____

_____

_____

Chapter Eleven:
Plummeting Standards

The parenting standards have plummeted in our country. The *CPCC Movement* believes one of the reasons this happened is because in the late '70s and early '80s, the parenting standards were not as they are now. This is because our parents had higher standards for us. They made us respect authority. We weren't permitted to question our parents. We had to get a job and help out around the house.

Some people, however, resented their parents for making them meet those types of standards. Some people disliked their parents for not satisfying all of their wants. In doing so, those people vowed to make sure their own kids had everything they didn't have. Unfortunately, they forgot one important part: to make kids earn their privileges. Television, iPads, smart phones, and video games are not things kids are entitled to. They are privileges, not a right. Instead, some parents gave their kids everything they wanted despite how the kids behaved. This mindset, though, was more for the parents' well-being, not the kids. Buying toys, name brand clothes, and electronics soothed the adult's feelings of guilt for not spending time with their kids, sorrow for missing out on milestones, and anger for being forced to work in order to give their kids everything. This started a vicious cycle. By spoiling their kids, it made many parents believe they were better parents to their children than their parents were to them. Today, the average kid doesn't believe they should work to earn the things they want or need. That mindset came because these youngsters were being given things they had not earned. Therefore, many of them developed an attitude that parents owed them things that older generations had to work hard to achieve. Hence, burglary, theft, robbery assaults, murders, and crime stats go up because these kids want things, and when life tells them to earn it, they don't understand what that means because they were never made to consistently earn anything. Not only have parents produced selfish kids, but the parents have robbed both adult and child of something far more important than material items. By not encouraging kids to earn their way in the world, those parents have taken away the pride and self-esteem generated from a job well done. Likewise, parents have robbed themselves of feeling proud when watching their children accomplish little steps and eventually climb all the rungs on this ladder called growing up.

In no way does the *CPCC Movement* imply that this is the only reason for kids acting out, but it certainly is a credible one. By changing the parent, the end result is the child will change as well. The *CPCC Movement* firmly believes that we have, not *the* solution, but *a* solution to correct this terrible mistake. The *CPCC Movement* can and will unite parents. The *CPCC Movement* will support, teach, coach, and inspire mass communication for parents everywhere. We can regain control while we re-teach entire families and change the present generation of children. But first, the parents have to be the ones to take that all important first step.

Think about it. By putting your foot down and saying, "No more!" and by applying the *CPCC* parenting standards, the children will have no choice but to comply. The kids can't support themselves. Everything they have comes from you. You, the parent, control everything right now. It's become easier to give in than to deal with fighting, debating, and arguing. If you are tired of being tired, it's time for you to check out the *CPCC Movement*. Thus far, your kids have been winning this battle, but this whole time, you've had the power to turn it all around. All it takes is for you to wake up and flip that switch.

Join the Movement!

Reflections

Chapter Twelve:

They Tried, But They Still Missed It!

Lately, I've noticed a number of men, with a considerable degree of celebrity status, make noble and honest attempts at correcting the problems with our youth. Although I have tremendous respect and admiration for their mindset and goals, I believe they still missed the main problem. Every program that I've seen on television, at penal institutions, or at schools focuses on the child. Everything is geared around putting the children in programs to correct their behavior. I understand this mindset because I began my mission in the exact same way–Fix the Kid...Fix the Kid!

Having said this, I will always have respect for anyone who is willing to stand up and try. I began working with kids over twelve years ago as a police officer. My involvement with them stemmed largely from police work centered on a wide range of crimes. Often, while processing kids, I would talk to them. "Why are you clowning around like this? Deep down, you seem to be a very nice young man." Time after time, I came to the same conclusion; basically, the environment at home was not conducive for their positive development. A few years later, I started volunteering at the juvenile detention facility in my community. I developed a program called "Man Talk." I believed then, and even now, that if I change the mindset, change the way human beings think about every aspect of their lives, they will change their own behavior. The "Man Talk" program was geared around changing the way those young men thought about their lives. I focused on altering their opinion of law enforcement, the meaning of family, relationships, and their long-term goals. This concept proved effective in changing the behavior of those juvenile inmates. You recall that this all took place inside the juvenile detention facility. An important part of this concept was that these young men were incarcerated for various lengths of time ranging from six months to years. They weren't in their homes but in a controlled environment.

Although a penal institution isn't a perfect representation of an organized, structured environment, it was more regulated than most of the homes these boys came from. In fact, it was also consistent, and their policies dictated that bad behavior would not be rewarded. Basically, these young men were in the type of environment we speak of in our book, *Change the Parent Change the Child!* This made it much easier to instill positive concepts that later evolved into "CPCC" into the minds of these young men. Over time, I could see these young men begin to change. They had hope, direction and purpose. They wanted to get out of jail so they could get it right this time. On numerous occasions, after being released, they would go home with these new ideas and concepts about their future. Their parents would want to meet me to thank me for helping their son. Many times, within minutes of watching and listening to the parents talking to their sons, I could clearly see how and why the kids were messed up. It wasn't long before I figured out why these young men would slowly regress back to their old ways not long after being released.

When the young men went back home, they were sent into the same unorganized, unstructured, inconsistent, bad-behavior-rewarding environment that ultimately landed them in the detention facility. Before long, the positive, upbeat boy who had left the facility bounced back with the same, if not worse, problems as before. I learned to ask the young men to leave my office so I could speak with the parents. I started coaching them on positive ways to interact with their sons. Soon, talking with the parents became part of the routine. Shortly thereafter, I was promoted to the rank of Chief of Police. Although I had many responsibilities in this new position, my passion for coaching parents only grew. I started spending more time coaching parenting skills.

Hence, *Change the Parent, Change the Child* was birthed. The main lesson I hope every parent understands is in order to change a child's bad behavior, the focus has to also be on changing the parents' bad behavior as well. The parents control everything in the children's lives. When parents bring their kids in for counseling or they want to report their children as being unruly, the first thing I ask is, "How did your child get this way? Has he always been unruly and disrespectful?"

In most cases, whatever problems the children had, the parents played a major role in helping them to evolve into "little monsters."

How do we fix it? How do we correct the behavior of this seemingly out-of-control youth?

Well, let's examine closely what we know and what has been proven.

1. Children are adaptable.

2. Children can adjust to pretty much any reasonable level or standard as long as the adjustment or standard is consistent and steadfast.

3. Children will meet or exceed society's standards when they are raised in an environment of love, compassion, discipline, organization, and structure. I would be remiss if I didn't include biblical and spiritual education.

When you look at all of these requirements, none of them can be obtained by the child alone. The one person who is in the position to provide this type of environment is the parent.

Having said all this, in my opinion, the answer to this problem is to improve parenting skills! If we shift our focus off of the child and direct it toward improving parenting skills, we all will win. When the environment at home changes, what choice do the children have but to adapt and embrace it? Where can they go; what can they do? Children can't, nor should they, provide for themselves. The parents provide everything in their lives, so they have no choice.

With this information in mind, think about these programs where the focus is on changing the behavior of the child by coaching and mentoring only the child. Imagine taking the child out of the negative environment at home for a three hour session of positive affirmation for three days a week. After each session, you take the child right back to the same mess that got them into trouble to begin with. At the very least, this will be a long, drawn-out process that usually ends up causing the children to have an even more negative opinion of their parents because, at the positive affirmation program, they see what they are missing at home, which can make them not like being at home even more. On the other hand, when the mindset of the parents change and they are empowered with the parenting skills from *Change the Parent, Change the Child,* then everybody wins!

Reflections

_____
_____
_____
_____
_____
_____
_____
_____
_____
_____
_____
_____
_____
_____
_____
_____
_____
_____
_____
_____

Chapter Thirteen:

Boxing Trainer vs. the Parent

Responsibilities:

There are many similarities in the responsibilities of parents and a boxing trainer. A trainer or coach has the responsibility of teaching his or her fighter all the intricate details of boxing. The trainer has to teach fighters how to defend themselves in the ring by blocking, parrying, or slipping punches. It could also mean throwing punches back, which could be a number of different types of punches. It's also important to be physically fit in order to use the skills you've learned. The trainer has the responsibility to teach the fighter all that I've said, and much more before he'll be ready to face an actual opponent. The more skills the fighter acquires, the better fighter he or she will be.

A good parent is quite similar to a good trainer. Parents are responsible for teaching their children the intricate details of becoming successful adults. Parents have to teach their children how to be successful in life by incorporating the human qualities of integrity, loyalty, truthfulness, honor, and humility. These are just a few of the human traits all parents should instill in their children. They have to be taught to apply these traits in their everyday decision-making. Parents have the responsibility to teach their children these traits and much more before they'll be ready to face the complex dynamics of adulthood. The more of these traits children acquire, the more prepared they'll be for what life will throw at them.

Cultivating a Winning Mind-Set:

The trainer has to cultivate an attitude often referred to as "Controlled Aggression" in his or her fighter. This means the fighter has to be able to control his anger in the ring and use it as fuel when things aren't going his way. Uncontrolled anger in the ring will cause the fighter to tense up, which will result in premature physical fatigue. The trainer has to cultivate a mindset of success in the fighter. In order to be successful, it is vital that the fighter believes he is capable of winning. Without that attitude, the fighter will be defeated before the first punch is thrown. A successful trainer will teach the fighter to never quit, no matter what. If you get knocked down, get back up; never stay down! This winning mentality will positively impact everything the fighter does, and will most likely stay with him throughout his life.

The same holds true for children. It is the parents' job to cultivate an "I can do it" thought-process in their children. Children need to be taught how to think positively in all things and to always believe they can achieve and accomplish their goals. In this process, parents have to teach children how to handle being told "no" when they believe the answer should be, "Yes." The time will come when life will knock them flat on their backs, and they will have to have a winning mind-set to get back up, to never quit–no matter what; like a nightmare, they just keep coming back! This winning mind-set will positively impact everything they do in life.

Sparring:

The trainer has to set up sparring sessions for his or her fighter. It is crucial that the trainer is careful in picking the right sparring partners for their fighters. In order to do this, the trainer needs to see how well his or her fighters' skills are developing. He doesn't want to see his fighters get beat up. So, he has to make sure the opponents do not overwhelm his fighters. During the sparring session, the coach is looking to see how well his pupil uses jabs, left hooks, right hooks, the defensive skills, and stamina. These issues all allow the trainer to know what to work on with each individual fighter.

Just like a good coach, parents need to prepare their kids by testing them periodically. Parents might consider testing the level of integrity in their children by leaving money visible and unattended to see if their children will take it. Another tactic might be to ask the kids a question that the parents know the answer to in order to test their honesty. These are tools parents may want to consider to gauge the development of those qualities in their children. If it is determined that there is a deficiency in any of those areas, it's time to go back to work. Ultimately, the objective is to prepare the child for the complex dynamics of adulthood.

The First Fight:

When the boxing coach believes it's time, he will sign the fighters up for their first fights. The instructor is nervous and concerned, probably even more so than the fighters because the trainer knows how important the first matches can be in determining what kind of fighters they will become. In some cases, the new fighter doesn't even realize the seriousness of the event. He's too excited to be in a match for the first time.

Similarly, when children turn eighteen years old, the parents will be nervous and concerned about what can happen when their kids start their first real job, go off to college or engage in a serious relationship. Most parents know from experience what can happen if things don't go well. Children are unable to foresee the consequences because they often are excited to experience new adventures.

Ultimately, if parents and coaches taught their charges all the skills they'll need, it should be an awesome experience for all concerned. On the other hand, if they haven't, children and boxers alike will suffer the consequences for the failures of the parents and the coaches.

Reflections

_____

_____

_____

_____

_____

_____

_____

_____

_____

_____

_____

_____

_____

_____

_____

_____

_____

_____

_____

_____

_____

Chapter Fourteen:

Appreciation

Appreciation is one of the most important ways to strengthen a relationship. At least once a month, I take time to reflect on my life and mentally acknowledge the people who have had an impact on me during that period. I call this my monthly life assessment.

In a relationship, it is imperative to appreciate everything your spouse or partner does for you. Often, it's the little things that mean the most. I enjoy receiving clothes, shoes, or new accessories for my Harley; however, what really makes me feel special are the little gestures in life. For example, I prefer evenings when my girl and I are sitting on the couch watching a movie while she's tucked in nice and tight under my arm, resting her head on my chest. Something as little as asking me if I would like something to eat or drink is meaningful to me.

I appreciate her loving me enough to want to get up and make me a sandwich or prepare a meal for me. Helping me study for an exam or reading my assignment aloud because I'm too tired to read it myself makes me feel special. These are examples of love, and like the old saying says, "You can't buy love." I'm grateful to have someone special in my life who loves and cares for me.

I often remember when I didn't have anyone to share life with. During my life assessment, I ask myself these questions:

1. Is my life better now that she is in it?
2. Do I feel better when she is with me?
3. Are my life situations easier to deal with since I met her?

This way of thinking reminds me to avoid becoming complacent and unappreciative. No matter how tough things may get at times, I always go back to those questions. If it gets to the point where I answer no to those questions, it may be time to step out of the game for a minute and reconsider my next move. It's always a good idea to sit down with the important people in life and have some serious conversations.

Both people in the relationship should focus on continually giving their spouse reason to admire, respect, love, and cherish them. Personally, I think one of the biggest causes of separation or divorce is complacency. Often, some people become so comfortable with their partners' loving and caring efforts–whether it is emotional or life-changing deeds–that they can delude themselves into believing that nothing can change–that all the things that they do to make life easier will never stop.

I refer to that as becoming complacent. In some cases, people might go as far as deciding they don't need that person who has done so much for them.

It is not until they're gone that they realize what they had, but by then, in most cases, it's too late. Now that they are alone, they can see things that others did to make their lives comfortable. Remember to always appreciate your spouse or partner.

Reflections

_____
_____
_____
_____
_____
_____
_____
_____
_____
_____
_____
_____
_____
_____
_____
_____
_____
_____
_____
_____
_____
_____

Shield & Buckler Coaching and Mentoring Inc.

9824 Washington St. Chagrin Falls, Ohio

Shield & Buckler Coaching and Mentoring offers instruction and techniques designed to improve life and living, by teaching cutting edge and doable concepts on parenting, team building/management, motivation, leadership and self improvement. Ultimately, the goal of S&B is to inspire human beings to become Better, Faster, Stronger human beings in all areas of life and living.

Here are previous books on parenting and for kids that are products of S&B:

"Change The Parent Change The Child"
"Why Do I Have To?"

We offer lectures, workshops, and parenting classes!
Be sure to like us on Facebook at Change The Parent Change The Child.

To contact S&B for more information or to set up an appointment go to:

www.myshieldandbuckler.com

www.ingramcontent.com/pod-product-compliance
Lightning Source LLC
LaVergne TN
LVHW040053090426
835513LV00027B/403